RACE

REBELLING AGAINST CRIMES AND EXPLOITATION

Published in Great Britain in 2022
by Big White Shed, Nottingham, England
www.bigwhiteshed.co.uk
Printed and bound by Imprint Digital, Devon

ISBN 978-1-915021-02-1
Copyright © Big White Shed
Cover Design by Raphael Achache

The rights of individual contributors to be identified as the authors of their work has been asserted in accordance with Copyright Designs and Patents Act of 1988, all rights reserved.

A CIP catalogue record of this book is available
from the British Library.

There are so many voices that need to be heard, stories to tell, and lessons that need to be learnt. This collection of voices, stories and perspectives speaks about racism, politics, history and women's rights. A light is shone on issues in a way that may not have previously been thought about. This book is an educational journey to improve knowledge and help shape the next generation.

Jay Sandhu 2021

CONTENTS

Introduction..6
Ain't Nothing Changed - Jay Sandhu..........................9
Where You From (inspired by Riz Ahmed) - Jay Sandhu......10
What They Think - Jaya Gordon-Moore......................13
Metamorphosis - Jake Davy..15
Britishness? - Jay Sandhu..16
Black History - Annie Alleyne.....................................18
Equality - Keiron Higgs...19
BLM - Sharmila McNulty-Sharma...............................20
#AllLivesMatter - Jay Sandhu.....................................21
Walk Like Me - Aalia Zorko...22
Poem 1 - Rasia Saghir...26
Raven with White - Jake Davy....................................28
On Socials - Jay Sandhu..30
I Feel Sick - Annie Alleyne..32
Who Am I - Keiron Higgs...33
Gammon - Jay Sandhu..35
To Boris Johnson - James Lamey.................................37
Liar Liar - Graham Lock...39
The Empire - Jay Sandhu..42
Stephen Lawrence - Andrew Martin...........................44
George Floyd - Andrew Martin...................................45
Liars and Bystanders - Sharmila McNulty-Sharma......46
Poem 2 - Rasia Saghir...47
People Hate Isms - Ferzana Shan................................48
Ode to Oligarchy - Kirsty Kellin-Lewin.....................49
The Culture - Jay Sandhu..53
Poem 3 - Rasia Saghir...55
Insert Kids Name - Jay Sandhu...................................56
Please Stop - Ferzana Shan..62

What is Privilege? - Jay Sandhu..........63
Enslaved - Annie Alleyne..........65
Eutopia - Sharmila McNulty-Sharma..........66
Will You Speak Out? - Keiron Higgs..........67
Traffic - Sharmila McNulty-Sharma..........69
Lewis Latimer - Stuart Whomsley..........70
Question From a Mate - Jay Sandhu..........71
Hey White Boy - David Fry..........74
"Colour Blind" - Hazel Warren..........76
Education - Jay Sandhu..........78
The End - Graham Lock..........80
Thanks - Jay Sandhu..........81

Writer Bios
Jay Sandhu - @Sandhuwrites..........84
Jaya Gordon-Moore - @JayaHadaDream..........85
Kerion Higgs - @keironhiggspoet..........86
Aaalia Zorko - @amzorko..........87
Andrew Martin..........88
Andrea (Annie) Alleyne..........89
Hazel Warren - @Hazeleypoos..........90
Ferzana Shan..........91
Kirsty Kelly-Lewin..........92
Sharmila McNulty-Sharma - @irisepoetry..........93
Raisa Saghir - @raisa1s..........94

INTRODUCTION

This project began back in the deep, dark, depths of the first lockdown... or it might have been the second one. Each time the country got plunged into restrictions, all of the days started to blend into one. I was inspired to put this poetry anthology together for several reasons. Partly because of the events surrounding Black Lives Matter in the UK and in the USA, and partly due to questionable acts by governments all over the world.

Throughout the pandemic, I have had important and informative conversations with family, friends and acquaintances on social media surrounding race. Discussions were happening for the first time about historical injustices and the concept of society. I was seeing people campaign for change, like Marcus Rashford fighting to feed kids. Even though I'm a lifelong Liverpool fan, I can give credit where it's due. A footballer in his early twenties doing the work of politicians, but still, they should stay in their lane... After the rollercoaster that was the Euros, seeing the hate he, Sterling, Sancho and Saka received after the final appalled me. I felt embarrassed to be technically English. My biggest achievement at 19 was a 35-kill streak on Call of Duty at shipment. Imagine having the weight of a nation on your shoulders, taking a penalty in a final.

At a local level during the pandemic, I saw people and organisations bringing about change and offering help like the Truth Mental Health, amongst others. For the first time, when teaching maths at a state secondary school, I saw kids having important discussions. They were asking what they should read to learn more, learn the truth, and how they can help make a change. It was great to have incredibly open conversations, ones that I certainly was never a part of at that age. I really am looking forward to the change the next generation will push through.

All of this was swirling around in my head, along with the conversations I was having about race. Themes started to emerge, and I thought that they needed to be collected and shared.

I also noticed a lot of both performative allyship and activism. People posting a black square on a random Tuesday without reading anything, watching anything, without buying independent or minority-owned. They just didn't want to be left out of the news cycle, or a social media trend. They need a bit of education, or to give enough of a shit to do something and stand up and be counted.

Rebelling Against Crimes and Exploitation is a collection of voices that need amplifying. These words will also hopefully give people an insight into experiences through another's eyes. It is here to educate ignorant people and encourage them to see past a single narrative. I want to see open and honest conversations in the mainstream media, in Parliament and in educational establishments. Hopefully, this will bring about some actual lasting change.

To help contribute to making a change, all profits made from this collection will go to The Black Curriculum. They are an organisation dedicated to educating young people to help create a better and more informed society. They do incredible work; you can check them out at theblackcurriculum.com.

Huge thank you to Anne Holloway and the team at Big White Shed for publishing this collection. It wouldn't have been possible without people that inspired this, everyone who submitted a poem and took time to write a piece for this collection and to everyone reading this.

Also, thanks to Megan Turner, who has spent hours editing this collection and correcting my bad grammar. As well as inspiring, motivating me and generally supporting me in every other aspect of my life, she rocks and is my rock.

To keep up with other things I am working on, you can find me at *@SandhuWrites* on socials. I also talk about a range of topics into a microphone. You can find it by searching for Jay Chats Podcast.

AIN'T NOTHING CHANGED - JAY SANDHU

Ain't nothing changed
The world's gone to shit
I really don't know what to make of it
So I'm sat at my table trying to find some words
To explain this irrationality, like I'm teaching surds
Searching for the perfect metaphor
Just wondering what for?

Ain't nothing changed
For all of us that are BAME
It's not just started happening
It's just starting to get filmed
People finally getting held accountable... well not really
George Floyd, Michael Brown, Breanna Taylor, Stephen Lawrence
Goes on and on, the list is endless
It's happening again and again

Ain't nothing changed
It's not just white privilege
Unconscious and institutional racism and bias
This shit repeats, it's historic
I bet it's nice not being targeted for just existing
It feels like we're in a fight and we can't swing back
Just take every hit and carry on because we're brown and black

We gotta make a change
It's time for us as a people to start makin' some changes
Let's change the way we eat, let's change the way we live
And let's change the way we treat each other
You see, the old way wasn't working so it's on us to do
What we gotta do, to survive

WHERE YOU FROM - JAY SANDHU
(Inspired by Riz Ahmed)

They ever ask you, "Where you from?" like, "Where you really from?"
The question seems simple, but the answer's kinda long
I could tell 'em Notts or Derby, but I don't think that's what they want
Won't tell 'em more, 'cause anything I say is wrong

When I say England, it's not what they want
Britain's where I'm born, and I love a cup of tea and that
But tea ain't from the UK, it's from where my DNA is at
And where my genes are from, that's where they make jeans and that
Then send them over to LDN, that's where they stack the P's and that

English, on forms, I never tick that box
Being British, I'd never brag
Skinheads got me walking quicker and if I see a Saint George's flag when it's not the World Cup
With tattoos of swastikas, not knowing its Indian origins
The Hindu symbol of good luck, but for some only associated with fear

Still getting angry when I'm at the receiving end of racism
But it's not even a tenth of what my Baba went through daily
In reality, it's not even a tenth of what my Grandad went through daily
And through all of that and he was always calm
We're still wanting to fight back, some heads I wanna crack
Some of these ignorant idiots need a smack
Would you blame us?

Generation after generation
Subject to diaspora
Then gentrification
Now having to protest a nation
Can you blame us?!
If we all came together, we'd build a new nation
Forgetting that you came and literally split our nation
Not only split but pillaged our nation
Then bought us…here to build their nation
I was raised by bhangra, grime, garage and halal Southern fried chicken shops

A junglist, a jungli, I'm Mowgli from The Jungle Book
Seeing me in Aladdin, realising it's a whole new world for us
We are making it, finally on TV, relating to that comedy
Big up Goodness Gracious Me
The racists can kiss my chudees, while I collect that cheque, please

Trying hard to assimilate, but at what cost?
Never once…did I want to be light, if I don't fit, forget you I don't give a toss
I see you making a quick judgement, my heritage you chose to toss
Never once…did I want to be light, it's my heritage you chose to toss

Physically, mentally, verbally attacked
By thick ignorant cats
Used to call me nerdy Pak
Drop an N-bomb then say I was dirty black
Never once got called a Jatt
If you didn't know that's my cast
I know it's outdated but that's my past
Uneducated morons living in the past

Sometimes I think would my life be easier
Living in India before the empire, you know in the past
Now air your opinion you finish first I'll finish last
My tribe is a quest to a land that was lost to us
And its name is dignity, so where I'm from is not your problem, bruv

WHAT THEY THINK - JAYA GORDON MOORE

Too black for the white kids,
...And too white for the blacks,
Do you know Marley had a black mum and a white dad?
I feel it in the one drop we were moved across lands,
Generational trauma trying not to feel sad.

They think because I'm lightskin that I'm rude and I'm bad,
Tony Blair Era - They think I grew up with chavs.
Curly haired yute with the dreams that you have,
Curly haired yute with a single mum and a staff.

I rap from a strong soul, so they start guessing my identity,
To assume I'm gay's a stereotype I've got no empathy,
I feel the glass ceiling trust we still ain't got no equity,
But I never let their bias break me down or get the best of me.

See everyone on free school meals was from the same area,
They tried to other us, moral panics, mass hysteria
Skin tone mysterious, so they get imperious,
"Oh you born in Cambridge? But you don't seem posh or serious".

Modern Day Mulato,
Strong mind but my heart's gold,
Folding any gatekeeper,
Who tries to box me in a tight mould.

No Blacks,
No Dogs,
No Irish
Trust me, I'm an Ital Paddy,
In slavery the Jezebel was just a piece of candy

Objectified, Raped, Sexualised
So when you fetishize me now,
How can I not get that vibe?

If I had a pound for every time someone said my skin was light,
A pound for every time they touched my hair without my right,
A pound for every time I got called nigga or too white,
I'd have a thousand pounds,
I guess I wouldn't be so tight...

METAMORPHOSIS - JAKE DAVY

When I was young I was treated stupid,
Like the ideas I had were insignificant.
Set on a path of ignorance, unable to break free.

But I studied my history.
And finally saw what it was I could begin to be.

The thoughts in my head were constrictive,
like the words in a bookcase.
Bound in the lies of authors, held captive;
Sealed away in duct tape.
Shackled
Concealing their deception;
A wretched fog.
A foul mist,
Hiding the truth of our excellence

But once this smog had evaporated

I could at last see,
My ancestors were scholars, intellectuals and kings.
It's time now for me to stand up
And let's see exactly what I was born to be.

BRITISHNESS? – JAY SANDHU

What is Britishness?
Apparently not me
I wasn't born with an opinion of the world
But it already had one of me
By seven racism was normal
By nine I understood I'd never be treated equally
I've been called all sorts
Al-Qaeda
Terrorist
Black illegitimate
Not British though
A Paki
A monkey
A nnn-nah you know what,
I ain't giving that phallus the satisfaction
Not letting them rent-free in my head
I'm gonna flip the script instead
Gonna use that pain to educate and explain
I've been called all sorts
Never British though

Even got asked why I (yes me) blew up the Twin Towers
Trying to explain the logistics of that at age eleven
But I'm so confused, how can I not be British?
Discounting the fact I was born here, as were my parents
And how you bought my grandparents

I mean you have;
A German royal family
A Norman ruling elite
A Roman/middle eastern religion
With Indian national dish
An Arabic/Indian numerical system
And a Latin alphabet

Yet you forget
A lot of you were Eastern Europeans or speaking Hebrew
The racists not realising the swastika is Indian too
Remember you'd have no empire if your army was all Mr Whippy, no flake
What about the 'British immigrants'? Sorry I mean expats

And I'm the one that needs to 'fuck off back home'

BLACK HISTORY – ANNIE ALLEYNE

Why is our history such a mystery?
Why is the truth of our lives, hidden in the archives?
The truth of our importance and influence,
Not readily available or historically referenced.

Why are our lives deemed less than others?
Less than other sons, daughters, fathers and mothers.
As a colour, black is all encompassing,
It absorbs and has the capacity to take in everything.
It's solid and strong, though depicted as evil and wrong.
It's authentic and true, its image needs a serious review.

So why only celebrate in Black History Month?
Like the rest of the year our stories don't count,
Or amount to anything January to September.
Like it's ok for people not to remember,
The struggles of our ancestors' lives …
And the millions of people who have died!

EQUALITY - KEIRON HIGGS

I am
3rd generation quarter Jamaican
With Irish blood
In the world I live in
I hope for more good
But we are surrounded
By constant
Separation.
I hope for the day we end this situation
For all race religion and orientations.
As we are the nation
Controlled by old fashioned traditions
Although they have been transitions
Hatred still gets the last word
And I find that absurd
As from what I was taught
From my own simple basis
No one is born homophobic
Or racist.
Love may be a four-letter word
But then again so is hate
They conflict, always up for debate
Who wins in the end?
I think it's a trend
That's it's decided in a draw
As people do not know how to be kind anymore.
So in this time of constant aural unrest
Educate yourself
Do your very best
As in my lifetime I wish to see
A world living together in equality

BLM – SHARMILA MCNULTY-SHARMA

And in the silence, she sang aloud 'The Lives of Black People Matter!'
So, he nodded in silent agreement.

And he saw they sank an old statue out of rage and frustration, so
He coined his own statement:
'British history matters'.

And he must not have known how British history is steeped in unjust, vile actions.

And he must not have thought about the loss of history in the lands now seen as 'attractions'.

What made Britannia 'great'
was the bloody riches looted from far away islands.

Is raid and rape, blackmail and take the history you crave to protect?

If not, you should rethink that caption.

#ALLLIVESMATTER – JAY SANDHU

You say all lives matter, because it's trending, it's "cool" being that guy
That opposes the consensus, we're not saying all lives don't
But at the minute it feels like all lives don't

You say all lives matter while walking past the homeless
Voting Brexit, demanding they go home, while ordering their kebabs

You say all lives matter, but you don't want to let in the war-torn refugees
Treating your cleaners subhuman

Horse's lives matter though
So, I take it you're vegan?

You say all lives matter
But you're uncomfortable calling Greg, Gina
While listening to her mention her husband
Or seeing Shabana in her "letterbox"
And general conversations about race

Yet somehow, you're comfortable with
Saying you understand their oppression
Not knowing your own history, uneducated
Complaining about looting when you taught us it
By coming to our countries and taking our shit

Yeah, you're right... all lives matter

WALK LIKE ME – AALIA ZORKO

We see people,
and we judge;
on how they present themselves.
The way they talk.
The way they walk.
How our eyes and minds perceive them -
we believe that to be true.
However we cannot always be sure of the secrets that lie behind the mind's eye.
-

My brother once told me
that I could be anything I wanted to be,
live how I wanted to live:
my life,
my choice.
But you see,
some things aren't always a choice.
You don't choose to walk the way you do,
naturally.
Your natural walk is your brain transmitting signals to your body to walk that
certain way.
-

Some things are
innate within us.
Biological.
Not perceived or learnt;
but hard-wired into our system.
The input is easy;
The output is hard.
We must realise that we cannot change the signals and the

code between the
input and the output,
otherwise the output becomes disjointed,
and,
incorrect.
We try to correct and we try to let out,
but what comes out isn't the truth:
it's a version of the truth we believe others want to hear,
not the truth we desperately want to let out.
-

I met this old lady once.
She told me about how she was campaigning for women's rights in the 1940s.
Another woman kicked her directly in the back.
Her back wasn't straight enough;
Nor her head high enough.
She struggled to walk properly after that.
And so, her walk changed.
Not by choice, but by oppression.
-

I had a hard time walking.
I can walk,
but it's hard to
walk
truthfully.
Being truthful to what my brain is telling me.
The input translating into the output;
I can't do it.
-

We are living in a world where truth is unknown.
Reputation needs protecting, but it is the lies that protect it not the truth.
We are scared of judgment, but will happily judge -

unjustified judgement.
Judgment based on false ideologies and belief systems that
are flawed.
And so, this leaves the oppressed down on their knees.
Oppression and discrimination hinders truth.
-

If I chose to take away your right to walk,
and instead had the power to leave you crawling
and hurting,
instead of letting you be:
how would you feel?
Flip that on its head -
If I took away your right to love:
what would you do?
-

Sometimes I'd like to walk like you.
In different shoes to my own.
I want to know what it's like to not be judged for how you
walk,
how you are
who you are,
really.
But it's hard to not care
about your judgement
and it really shouldn't be
-

hard
but when people find out that you're...
That makes you
a completely different person.
 – No. I am still me.
Someone you pass in the street.
I am still your daughter.
Your friend.
-

Your sister.
I am [blank*].
And I am still afraid to say that.

* The reader must choose a word that fits with themselves to fill in the blank. What makes you different? What is something that you are still afraid to say?

POEM 1 - RASIA SAGHIR

And can you tell me if I am wasting time?
With this stress on my mind?
I can't live this life no more, I can't even grind,
When you don't get no signs that this life is going to get better.
And my world is so cloudy, in dark ass weather,
Whenever someone passes, it's the only time we're together,
I know you know how I feel, because all the motherfuckers; they've been acting different,
They only check up when you're in the casket.
Listen, they keep on switching up,
And even you know that when they're gone; they are really gone,
You know you can do better because everyone's got flaws,
But they don't care about you,
It only benefits them and if it doesn't then fuck you,
They don't keep you safe, they want to make the shit spread like it's peanut butter.
So when you're going to go please don't come back,
You've got to work right out because the struggle is real hard,
But you've got to chill out,
We're going to work and work it out until,
And we'll keep on stressing, until the day we're out of this drought.
And I'm climbing to the top because that's my only way out,
But if I finish I am not tripping,
I don't wanna live with a doubt,
And I don't care about stacking a hundred,
I only care about the people that will be here when I'm running around,
But if I catch you fucking around, I'm going to jump your ass

and leave you with a blast,
I never spoke on your name and if I did then you didn't want it,
So fuck it,
Go get down on your knees.
You only always listen to lies and I only listen to me,
You're only worried about clout and I am only worried for me,
Because I am all up alone and I don't get nothing for free.

RAVEN WITH WHITE - JAKE DAVY

I still remember the moment I realised my skin wasn't like my mum's.
It's a strange epiphany for a four year old,
She hugged me close. Told me that, some people looked different. But inside we're the same.
She told me never to judge.

It wasn't so many years later;
Singled out by my peers,
the crow born with white feathers,
Chased and pecked for their differences.
Less time still before being called a nigger,
a coon or a wog.
Kids don't know what's hidden behind those words.
And yet still the intent is clear
Nor were those who are meant to educate me exempt.
I was like Polaris; the brightest star of my class.

Overlooked, neglected and put down. Suddenly the North Star feels more like a black hole,
absorbing everything but letting nothing show.

Times has passed, the years turned to decades;
You can still see those scars, on my knuckles, my face and my spirit.
Like jagged wounds dug in a cliffside.

Even now I can't walk down the street with my white girlfriend.
Not without the looks,
seething stares burning breaches into my soul.
Still I hear the names, those slanderous slurs
the aggression is still there; the same hatred festering beneath the surface.

You see, I was taught to love,
to love everyone.
Wholeheartedly and without reservation.
But it seems some people skipped that class,
Sometimes I think, it will never end.

But there are those.
The beautiful few.
Who give me hope,
for a better tomorrow.

ON SOCIALS – JAY SANDHU

On socials trying to explain about racism,
Becoming a keyboard warrior, feeling like a qwerty Viking,
Taking on the trolls, trying to get into social Valhalla,
Feeling like we're heading to our own Ragnarök,
This is getting ancient, it's 2020 and not 940.
Brothers will fight and kill each other,
No man will have mercy on another,
But I gotta keep calm, like Akala and George,
I can't be the angry ethnic, offended at your stupid ill-conceived little comments,
Trying to explain institutional, historic and systematic in a tweet,
Waiting for their 'well thought out' reply,
It might not sound like it, but I've got facts and diction,
Attempting to break down the deep-rooted causes of racism,
About why some feds seem fine clipping,
All over levels of melanin,
You forced the door shut for 400 years,
Then eventually let them in,
Only to use Rosewood to stoke your privilege,
Because you didn't want them to come up,
So you made yourself the opps,
Opposition, oppressors, destroyer of opportunities,
I think they'd rather take their chances with Beerus,
Because you know the food bangs, they be safe,
Institutional, historic and systematic issues got me doubting myself,
Making us think we only got the job because we're the BAME hire,
"There he goes playing the race card again"
Woah, hold up, ask yourself why is the 'race card' that colour?

You haven't had to let racism become normal and just brush it off.
We got 99 problems and I'm tired of brushing that dirt off my shoulder,
What more can I say?
There's a lot of facts you don't know and won't hear today,
All because it doesn't feed into the media's optics or rhetoric,
Algorithms just perpetuating your already outdated story,
Apparently, there'll be fewer hearts if your feed showed a different view,
Learning the truth? Now that's up to you,
Take your time, research and educate,
Let's turn things around, I know it already feels too late,

Let's make sure the next generation doesn't need to protest.

I FEEL SICK – ANNIE ALLEYNE

I feel disgusted!
I feel shocked!
I feel sick!
Sick, like I've been whipped!
Whipped by The Man, the Whip Hand and the history books,
My heritage of Pride and Industry shook.

I'm repulsed by the thought of sugar passing my lips,
Knowing its sweetness hides such bitterness.
Imported to mask the taste of coffee and tea,
It created an industry where people were not free.

Not free to live the lives they were meant to,
But instead enslaved and treated like cattle.
Punished for wanting to just be,
Free from a life of slavery.
Free from cruelty, sadism and racism.
Free from the cane fields, the Masters and capitalism.

I feel anger towards the pioneers,
Who bought my ancestors to progress their careers.
I feel sadness that profit and loss
Were deemed more important than the lives that they cost.

I'm tormented by visions of shackles and branding irons,
The copper manilla traded for people's lives.
The brutality, torture and pain, though legally abolished, still remain...
in the pages of books and records of history
Revealing an industry that treated people like property.

WHO AM I - KEIRON HIGGS

My families would've travelled on boats
from places far away
they could've gone anywhere
but in this town, they'd stay

Two second-generation kids
who met on the CB
was the start of the conception
of me.
My mum was a Punk
my dad was a Ted
both from different backgrounds
that much to be said

One from Pellon
The other from Queen's Road
Halifax was their humble abode
As one half of the family is Jamaican
the other with Irish roots
I was born with both these attributes
But as both heritages
have meant a lot to me
I'm Yorkshire born and bred
as far as the eye can see.

Who Am I?
A suede head
Crombie boy in size 7 DM shoes
from the same aisle as Ted Hughes
A Halifar-gone-ian,
born and bred

Jamaican Irish

but has no accent
nor no dread
A child with both parental last names
not known to many
but a unique select few
As the "bard of Halifax"
Keiron Lee Higgins
that'll do!

GAMMON – JAY SANDHU

Oh?! You want me to rap about injustice and civil unrest,
How about all the colours that get wrongfully arrested,
Injustice?! A fucking joke?! I don't know where to start.

Maybe somebody's life got taken and now somebody is missing a heart,
What happened to settling disputes on Mario Kart,
No? Instead, kids in primary walking around with steel,
Solution? Take the plastic knife out of their chicken box meal.

Oh shit?! Replace it with an inspirational story,
Bullshit! Just has me wondering who benefited from that deal,
I'll tell you who? Probably a mother fucking Tory!

Blood spraying back and forth,
And all you're worried about is your blue passport,
Somebody needs to use their brain to improve the issues way up north,
But all you want to do is put these kids in court.

How about we reinvest that money to educate,
Prevent instead of react,
Teach instead of incarcerate,
Address the problems, no need for a strap.

More opportunities are needed,
Or we're just creating a vicious cycle,
Maybe then we can stop the yute dem bleeding.
Don't live up to the stereotypes, that's archetypal,
Otherwise, each generation this shit just be repeating,
To fix the world, might need some black magic,

maybe juju J should be my alias,
It's not the culture, it's the government that's failing.

TO BORIS JOHNSON – JAMES LAMEY

You're Frankenstein meets floppy hair,
You play with lives, yet you don't care,
You're the maker and the monster
Of the hate that hurts and haunts her.

Tell me why you have to hurt her
When she only wears a burkha,
Woman, mother, sister, wife
She just wants to live her life.

Though you call it male oppression
Sometimes it's her free expression
If it is the woman's choice
Where's your right to gag her voice?

And it is such hypocrisy
With all your infidelity
To take a swipe at Muslim men
When you betrayed your wife again

Does it mean your girlfriend's free
When she screams out 'Get off me!'
Aren't you just like other men
Showing who's in charge again?

I hate it when they say your name
And play their bullshit Boris game
So listen Johnson, this is true,
Here's the damage done by you!

'She looks like a pillar box'??
What you said puts back the clocks
Hitler, Goebbels, Mosely, Powell,
Did the same as you do now.

When you say it, it seems right
If you've nothing and you're white,
Living on some dark estate
Looking for someone to hate.

Then neglect and poverty
Made worse by austerity
Help to make your poison flow
And your monster starts to grow.

How can you be prime minister
When you've done things so sinister?
When you hurt the innocent
Don't say that it was never meant!

For when she's walking down the street
It is your monster that she'll meet
That shouts the insults which are said
That rips the burkha from her head

And when she's fighting for her life
They'll be your prints upon the knife!

LIAR LIAR – GRAHAM LOCK
(with apologies to William Blake)

Liar! Liar! orange bright,
Beacon for the ultra right,
What immodest boast or lie
Could TRUMP your own mendacity?

On what distant golf course green
Did you learn to strut & preen?
Whence the bragging? Whence the bile?
Whence that vain & faux hairstyle?

And what migrant plea or groan,
Could hope to crack your heart of stone?
And when your tiny brain goes live
How can common sense survive?

Putin's creature? Wall Street's tool?
Or just a pussy-grabbing fool?
Will saying it in every tweet
Ever make your shit smell sweet?

When the stars in horror shrink
From the depths to which you sink,
Will you still shield your tax return?
And fiddle while your cities burn?

You put all heaven in a rage,
Keeping babies in a cage!
Sexist! Racist! Half-insane!
Führer of your country's pain!

Off to Florida you go
With your Stepford wife in tow,
Shoot the breeze & play some holes,
Forget about the melting poles.

The seas may rise, the skies may drop,
To you, the pole's a strip-joint prop.
You'll rue the climate smarts you lack
When that breeze starts shooting back.

Your mother groan'd! Your father wept!
To raise a leader so inept!
Who stokes white hate, who stirs white fear,
And treats black lives as just small beer.

Is that a Bible in your paw?
Would you besmirch all faith & law?
Do you believe a prophet's look
Can mask the profiteering crook?

Now thousands die & nations grieve,
Still you bluster & deceive,
Spouting twenty thousand lies
That bolsters COVID's deadly rise.

So re-election's all you craved,
With COVID filling every grave?
And now you've lost, you sulk & flounce,
As if your ego's all that counts?

Sack him! Sack her! Take no blame!
Throw a tantrum, stare down shame.
Railing as you lose your grip,
Like Ahab on his sinking ship.

And now you're desperate for Plan B,
Let loose the dogs of anarchy—
Civil war? Or nuke Iran?
Apocalypse - is that your plan?
You'd risk killings to escape
Standing trial for fraud & rape?
Afraid a youthful harlot's curse
Might further blight your marriage hearse?

Why tell Proud Boys to stand by?
Why turn from every Black Man's cry?
Your white supremacy appals,
& runs in blood down White House walls!

Pardon cronies, though they're crooks?
No matter how corrupt it looks?
Yet executions are rushed through —
Guess those guys never worked for you!

You've tainted and defiled so much,
Democracy shrinks from your touch.
Now your fate looks less than swell —
To rot in gaol, then burn in Hell!

Liar! Liar! orange bright,
Frontman for the fascist right,
What deluded boast or lie
Could TRUMP your vile hypocrisy?

THE EMPIRE – JAY SANDHU

The Empire, Churchill, Pro-Trumpers, Brexiteers, White Privilege and Fragility,
That shit makes me not like white people,
But I'm not racist, some of my best friends are white.

I get it you're annoyed, about something you had no control over.
Ill-reported history, that ends up making your people look worse than are, almost beastly,
Sounding familiar?
You're getting more annoyed, about things that happened across the world than on your front door,
But you showed that black square of solidarity, so you did your bit and all calm,

Let's take it back and explain this empirically,
How about I come to your house,
Steal your shit, fuck your wife, confuse your kids,
I mean leave your house intact, but the home's broken,
Then give you a token, of representation,
Your families are now divided, fighting, over that Kashmir jumper, that you used to be happy sharing,
Then after that, I go to your cousin's, your neighbour's and do that again and again,

Oh, then you'd say: 'but if we didn't invade, you would of',
Pfftt bullshit, we were more civilised,
More educated, had more wealth, better strategies but chose to live in our lane,
Now imagine a world where we had overtaken,
I doubt it, but you might be out on the streets saying white lives matter,

Or maybe, just a hypothesis... this world would be doing much better.

The Empire, Churchill, Pro-Trumpers, Brexitiers, White Privilege and Fragility,
That shit makes me not like white people,
But I'm not racist, some of my best friends are white...

STEPHEN LAWRENCE – ANDREW MARTIN
(13/09/74 - 22/04/93)

Stephen, loved in life
locally in London,
your name now a global reference
for our capital city,
when knives are used,
where lives are lost.

Blades and blame,
human and social costs,
public services slashed.
Each fatality, someone's
brother, daughter, sister, son.

People choose to settle scores,
no winners, only losers,
urban drug turf wars.

Funding cash cuts.

Final breaths, further deaths,
scars are lines not to cross.

GEORGE FLOYD – ANDREW MARTIN
(14/10/73 - 25/05/20)

Need to check police training,
knee to neck, breath straining,
plea to stop, pulse waning.

Need to check white supremacy,
greed is global, immediacy,
freed from slavery, history?

Racism pandemic, no vaccine,
no isolation, need to socially
distance from prejudice.

Taking a stand, taking a knee,
stand for something or
fall for anything.

Another son bites the dust,
twenty dollars fake note,
cheap price on black man's life.

LIARS AND BYSTANDERS
- SHARMILA MCNULTY-SHARMA

A swarm of wasps
stung the air
Violating the wind
Poisoning the ears
Of the vulnerable.
Their disease spread
And the bees hovered
Silently debating
Watching and appropriating
The ways of old.
The same story is stung
And each time
The wasp tongue
Grows stronger.

POEM 2 – RASIA SAGHIR

'Aurat muhabbat toot kar karti hai,
Intezaar bhi karti hai,
La'parwahi, sab kuch bardash karti hai,
Lekin jab ek aurat eik dafa parwah karna chor de toh ap chahe uske,
Qaadmon mein gir jao,
Woh parwah nahi karti'

(translation)
A woman loves brokenly,
She patiently waits,
Carelessly, she tolerates everything.
But, when a lady is broken and nothing affects her anymore; then you want her,
You'll fall to your knees,
Because she doesn't need you.

PEOPLE HATE ISMS - FERZANA SHAN

Racism, sexism, terrorism
but worst of all feminism

Feminists are seen like terrorists
They have demands
Not a demand for power and terror
But a demand for fairness and presence

The feminists waving their placards
fighting for their rights
Seen like terrorists brandishing their knives
fighting for their rule and might

The feminists fighting the invisible bogeyman
Misogyny and patriarchy
These are neither men nor man-made
But systems held in place stitch by stitch
A patchwork of beliefs, ideas and rules
A comfort blanket for all to stay under

But not the feminists
They step out
Men and women
Creating their own quilt
A patchwork of new beliefs, ideas and rules
No demonising of men here
No undermining of women
All welcome
As long as you don't hate the Ism of feminism

ODE TO OLIGARCHY - KIRSTY KELLIN-LEWIN

How many men
How many many men?
Not a vocal warm up
Vocal cords cut
Lower class torn up
Suppin till guts rot
Fucked like porn smut
Your love uncut...Pure but...

Arrogance strut strut
Coked up wankers.

No clean cut, clear cut,
cut with shit cuts,
cheap like peanuts,
Price so ruinous
Cut with shit
Fuck, make your head rush,
Bent like walnuts.
Straight like robots.

Arrogance strut strut.
Coked up wankers.

How many men
How many many men?
No vocal warm up
Throats are clean cut
Bridges leapt off
Lethal pills scoffed up
Train tracks fall off
Hanging like so rough
Childhood so tough

Life so messed up.

Arrogance strut strut
Coked up wankers.

Stats recorded
Lives so sordid, morbid,
Emotions boarded
up

Like shut shops
Lines till nose pops
Limp like cock flop
Lines like raindrops
Wash away deep cuts
Soak with pissed
Up coked up drugged up
Running cos guts rot
Stuck in this rut rut
Drop more pills but
Nothing can stop stop.

Arrogance strut strut
Coked up wankers.

Neck more shots back,
Necks on train tracks
Shot some brains - whack
Spinal cord snap snap.
Feel your life crack
Pipes like icing
Whiteness blinding

Life so frightening
Feel the noose tightening
Up

Like cords and ropes
The joke's
On you. What to do. No clue.
You're blue.
Shot through

Screwed.
Up like paper.
Voiceless narrator
Silent translator
Grief generator?
Truth negator?
Tired troublemaker?
Vile vindicator?

Meet your maker
Incinerator.

Burnt.

Like waste
Pour petrol on your face
This disgrace
Have no place
to go
No emotions show
Just weary
Vision bleary
You see death so clearly.

Exhausted
Pipes, car windows
Ignition so fumes blow
Out your breath,
blow
Up like semtex

Fucked like rough sex
Nothing but stress stress
Time to decompress
End this big mess
Gasp your last breath.

How many men
How many many men
Must die again again again?

Arrogance strut strut
Government funds cut.

THE CULTURE – JAY SANDHU

I've not got a problem with you saying you listen to rap and grime
But I have got a problem with you wasting my time
Explaining, to me, its idiosyncrasies
Explaining, to me, why they sell keys
Especially when you don't know Nasty or Mo Fire crew
Oi! Greazy talk doesn't equate to brainless
Privilege only applies if you BAME-less
Oi! Rapping don't lead to crime
People made it out without a rhyme
Also I said Nasty, not Narstie
That's Natural Artistic Sounds Touching You
Ready to school us, but it's Class of Deja
You think you know us, cause now we're on the TV
Finally getting representation, more than Goodness Gracious Me
And not just news or Crimewatch, we got our own gig
Narstie, Riz & Guz doing it big!
Tonight I'm the master of this ceremony,
This ain't my dissertation this is my testimony,
Everything I say straight truth, no phoney,
I have been listening to bars since I was making picture frames with macaroni,
Open an ear, my influences, you might just hear,
Listening to Nas and Biggie wearing baby gap,
I'm doing this for the art, the love of rap.
Doing it my style because I don't like trap,
Too many people are uneducated, quick to judge,
Outdated views, negative stigma we can't seem to budge,
Hears rap and go straight to gangster crap,
And you know what? Fuck them and fuck that,
This culture is way more than opportunities.
Well actually there for a lack

Simply being brown or black
Glorifying guns and a big back
Shottin, tut, my bad, I mean selling crack
Getting out and not going back.
If you don't get it, don't judge, just stop look and listen,
Otherwise you're deaf and blind, the whole point of this game, you're missing,
It's not just about stunting and seeing your watch glisten,
Man out here creating their own rules like it's Monopoly,
That's calm we can play, as long as;
If you lose, you don't flip the board angrily,
Remember should be assisting, lifting each other up, all love like Klopp and Bobby,
People spending most of their life on the ropes like Rocky,
Or worse still getting shot down like riiiicccckkkkyyyyy,
I know you think we all blaze and are thick as shit
Thinking we're the reason for the bullet holes in our ribs
Like we didn't want to grow old and have kids
Macaroni frames with their pics
Dave, Akala, Simz and Kano
Just to name a few
That speak with eloquence and grace
You might not hear it cause they say it at pace
Each album is like an entire bookcase
They taught me to be introspective
Maybe, you'd listen more,
If I said they were poets like me or George?
Or? You realise they are talking history, being all wretchrospective
Honestly, I think it's great you're trying to help
But, maybe your energy is just misplaced
Let's redirect and not waste
These artists and story weavers
Don't listen to how it's said
Listen to what is said
Then maybe, just maybe, we can start making a difference.

POEM 3 – RASIA SAGHIR

Tonight feels like the worst night of my life,
My world is ending,
Why can't I do one thing right?
Except this form of self expression,
Every breath I take is painful,
Shit went left and now I'm lost direction,
Now I'm left with nothing, just a twisted lie and my reflection,
Fuck a happy ending,
This real life, no fabrication,
I wake up tired, I wake up dead inside,
I have no motivation.
My mind and my body is divided,
I can't handle this separation,
I can't even hide it,
Every word I write is a contemplation.
Look at my body, it's really covered in scars,
Lighting a blunt and I fly with the stars,
I'm living in a world of my own, my Mars, all of my secrets that tear me apart,
I'll always be in the dark,
This isn't a beat, it's the beat of my heart.
I haven't got nothing to prove,
I know what'll happen when I'm on track,
I'm putting nails in my coffin,
Let me remind you I'm back,
Better late than never but I'm sadder than ever.
Depression and tears - making me crack,
Cold nights in December, I'll make you remember.
The feelings in trying to leave in the past.

INSERT KID'S NAME – JAY SANDHU

Met the girl, year 7 first day of term,
Immediately my attention was drawn,
Had that short, blonde, Captain Marvel hair-do
Thought she would've got more stick,
Her character was big, didn't even need to deal with it,
Told in advance she's got bare problems at home,
After speaking, all she wants to do is learn,
Lively in class but at breaks sits alone,
Seemed on the right path but could easily turn,
One day at break I asked if she's ok,
She said 'sir I'm good sometimes I just like tranquillity'.
Don't know what it was but saw pain and sadness in her eyes,
But, the future made her smile,
'Can't wait to leave, get out, it's going to be lit when I hit University'.
Then I saw the marks, asked if she's good,
'Sir I know it's bad but I just wish he dies'.

Bruv.

My heart sunk,

That shit got me feeling dead inside,
Doing what I can to keep her spirit alive,
Don't want to see that short blonde do, laid to rest in a far too small casket,
Don't want her to be a memory or just another story about lost potential,
Don't want to be at a funeral for this Queen, this Captain,
Or see the death of her marvel,
So, I found her a drama club, somewhere she can get lost inside,

Said that acting's an escape and she wants to be on Broadway,
'Trust I'ma smash it, film and TV, you'll see me like every day...'

And you know what 5 years later...
I saw her killing it on BBC

I don't know how to help, should I get involved,
We're told as long as they get a 4 or 5 that's their problems solved,
I'm there trying to do more, trying to improve their life,
Don't want them to meet their end with a gun or knife,
Don't want to catch their body cold like them Eskimos,
Shit, it's year 11, into the real world it's time to go

I used to try think of bars on the way to work,
Went out one night and saw a girl I used to teach tryna twerk,
Won't use her name but, we'll call her Mary,
That's my little clicker,
For me this story, it's a bit scary,
She had a little tick, most wouldn't've clocked,
When she's scared or nervous, out of sight she'll click,
Told me in detention, that's when we clicked,
'Sir...I know I got a detention, but you're sound, why does every uvver teacher treat me like shit?'

I was speechless, didn't have an answer to that,
Bonded over music, but not the ones that were "hits",
The ones that made a 12-year-old girl not fit,
Now I'm in the club getting stressed and shit,
It was like detention with a difference,
She didn't see me, but I clocked her doing a couple of lines,
At school, she was vulnerable at the best of times,
Now hanging with people that's not best for her life,

I hope she remembers all I taught her,
All the chats we had, hope she gets sorted,
I hope none of these fuck boys around her are extorting,
Then when they left for the bar, that's when Mary started clicking.
Those fuckboys just walked past me.
I overheard what they were planning
To do and make her do,
Known her since this big, watched her grow,
Put in years of effort, now don't know how to get involved,
Supposed I might just have to let this one go,
Could take her to rehab but sometimes those doors just revolve,
This shit pisses me off, good girl, now spinning out of control,
At school started as a Magikarp, put in bare time couldn't wait to see her evolve,
Years of training and levelling up, waiting for her to hit her Gyarados flow,
But truth be told, we might never know,
I spent too long debating, turned around, now my little clicker's gone, Abra-Kadabra-Alakazam teleport, gone, disappear,
Hopefully not more lost potential on a green and blue sphere,
I'm scared for Mary,
The not knowing, that's the part that is so scary.

I don't know how to help, should I get involved,
We're told if they get a 4 or 5 then that's their problems solved,
I'm there trying to do more, trying to improve their life,
Don't want them to meet their end with a gun or knife,
Don't want to catch their body cold like them Eskimos,
Shit, it's year 11, into the real world it's time to go

On a level, I'm not trying to preach,
All I do all day is teach,
Kids from both sides of the track,
Trying to make a difference trying to give back,
But fuck; the systems are broken.
Some kids fighting against a pack,
That's constantly stacked,

This one is about that lad that always rocked a blue Adidas bag,
He pretty much rocked it from year 7 through to 11,
The only bag he had with a tag,
The only dad he knew rocked a tag,
Positive male role models, never had,
School was hard and ADHD made it bad,
Teachers don't understand still giving little man grief,
With him, never had a chat, doesn't know at home. little man's chief,
Mum's off her head on more than just weed,
Dad for years, like he's never been seen,
Little man wants no stress at school, just a slate to be clean,
Not only that, everyday little man gotta pick up brother and sis,
Feed, bath, help with homework with all that shit,
And oh yeah get GCSEs,
I want to help but I only see him two hours a week,
So I have a laugh, he's naughty but I let few things slide,
Coming to math. I know he likes it. But out loud he only says 'sir you're alright',
I tell him your life ain't easy don't give up you'll have to fight,
A few months I'll never see him again,
I hope he doesn't end up shot down like Michael,
Hoping he stays outta trouble, breaks the cycle,
Now little man. Just turned 1-6,
Little, nah I mean big man not even 5'6.

I don't know how to help, should I get involved,
We're told as long as they get a 4 or 5 that's their problems solved,
I'm there trying to do more, trying to improve their life,
Don't want them to meet their end with a gun or knife,
Don't want to catch their body cold like them Eskimos,
Shit, it's year 11, in the real world it's time to go

Weekday no school today,
But no cheer no whoop today,
Black trouser with the crease,
White shirt, black blazer,
Need that Kleenex in the pocket g,
Needed the whole box last week,

He was 14, whole life left, shits peak,
Life's gone, another dad missing a son,
Mixed up in the wrong shit,
Ended up the wrong end of a gun,
He was a good kid, just easily led,
Trying to roll with the mandem acting like a big lad,
Now the whole school and more out in this field,
It's raining but that could just be the tears,
The yungen was set to go Oxbridge,
Wanted that Stormzy scholarship,
Shocked us all, not one indication of wanting to roll deep or carry a clip,

Turns out wasn't even rolling,
Wrong place, wrong time, wrong clothes, wrong bag,
He just fit a description,
He was a bit autistic,
But he always listened,
When he could hear,
Not with all the sirens near,
For his life, he didn't gone fear,

And what sounds like "put your hands behind your head"
Was actually "don't fucking move and we won't have to shoot"

Used to be scared about this happening,
He did what everyone told him to do,
Bro listen if they stop you

Do as they say

Put your hands up

You'll be ok G

But he wasn't, was he?

PLEASE STOP – FERZANA SHAN

You tell me we're equal
Then say the king size mattress is bigger than the queen size

You tell me we're equal
Then ask if I'm Miss, Mrs, or Ms

You tell me we're equal
But give me less pay so he can have more

You tell me we're equal
But say the king-size room is better than the queen size room

You're telling her she's equal
Then give her a toy pram and him a toy gun to play with

Please Stop

WHAT IS PRIVILEGE? - JAY SANDHU

My first attempt to write in a bop but no Stormz, vossi,
This is about the police stopping me,
Under this, covid, half locked, UK,
I went for a run in the sun today,
The 5-0 van pulled up, 3 times, glaring,
But the other bunch of runners, no melanin, no staring.

What is privilege?

This shit had me reaching for my phone,
Like This is America, hoping the police don't take that tone,
Loading a live stream, just in case,
Might've been nothing, but head's spinning straight to worse case, Don't know if it's media or socials that's got it twisted,
I just don't wanna see the blue light and my skin tone getting wrongfully lifted, Let's be fair the leaders aren't helping, that's both sides of the pond,
Maybe it'll change when Idris or Kano become Bond.

What is privilege?

Two or three months into 2020 and I've already had more casual racism than in the last 10 years,
Leaders dropping travel bans, Chinese viruses, piccaninnies and letterboxes to feed fears,
Getting called Mohammed and a terrorist, like it's normal at the end of the night out,
Still getting called a Paki, thick mutha fuckers ain't even got the country or religion right,
Since 2001 shit has been getting worse, not better
Hopefully, the kids of today can fix it, influence it and be a trendsetter.

What is privilege?

It's pretty much the whole gov going to the same school,
Misrepresentation in plenty sectors, ain't many teachers that look, sound and act like me,
It's not getting confused when in your rice and peas, you get kidney beans,
Not getting ripped for ordering a korma,
It's understanding every grime reference - budabopbop and sounds of sir,
It's there not being enough role models to represent our culture,
Nodding to people you've never met because somehow, they understand too,
It's before you even speak, people's perception of you,
Being locked down with a yard, heating, water and food,
It's not being locked down somewhere you feel unsafe,
It's having all your limbs, the ability to think,
It's not having to need,
It's being born into,
Something you can't earn,
It's a commodity,
It should be a thing of the past,
But honestly, I think it's here to last.

ENSLAVED – ANNIE ALLEYNE

Caged, enraged and enslaved!
Men, women, children and babes!
What did they do to deserve such ill treatment?
Beaten, whipped, raped ... completely abhorrent.

What could they do to escape their plight?
Speak out, rise up, revolt and fight?
No, not that easy, though their numbers were many,
Those in power knew how to protect their pennies.
Terrorise, dehumanise and weaken their black cattle,
So they'd cower in fear rather than contemplate battle.

Those in charge knew exactly what they were doing...
They devised instruments of torture to prevent financial ruin.
Business came first, money and then property.
No time for reflection, compassion or morality.

EUTOPIA – SHARMILA MCNULTY-SHARMA

A world without crime

In the summer season
Doors were swung open-wide
The breeze that drifted inside, warm and clean.
The streets buzzing with euphoria
The roads gently humming with intent.

Even an autumn here is spent
Latches unlocked, dark evening walks,
The laugher of young girls in the park
And gathering golden leaves ready to pile.

The only blade felt this winter is from the icy cold,
The only shots are those of a thrown dart or scattered stone.
No harsh words resort in fire or blood on our floors.

And, in the spring, community is reborn,
We laugh to scorn the barbaric past
Of war and revenge or attack
When the lambs arrive there's no going back
To what inhumanity came before.

WILL YOU SPEAK OUT ? - KEIRON HIGGS

You can pull down the statues
Take back all that's been said
But you'll never sever
the racist hydra head
I'll scream blue murder
Attack it with my fists
But it will not stop
The fact it still exists
Because the world
Is ran by right wing views
If I don't read it in a paper
I see it in the news
And Racism doesn't die.
It just goes back under
And in this time I really do wonder
Why I should have a say at all.
Then I remember this:
Have you ever been called
A black b-stard
A n-gger
A coon
ever seen your race depicted in an unfunny cartoon
Because I have
But It's all considered yano, funny banter
But now it's time to listen to this Haligonian ranter:
This is England 2020
Home of bullshit patriots plenty
The man claiming how he doesn't like the Irish, the black nor the brown
Whilst supping his Guinness
Eating a curry
And dancing to Motown
Blacks lives matter

And Human beings matter
But my head is feeling like it's taking a batter
Fighting among ourselves
To reach the biggest issue
Like who do these causes
Really permit to?
But I'm forever mentally flying
My flag of red black and white
As I refuse to be trampled by the rise of the right
It may be popular to speak out aggressively
But it's more better to see
People striving
For racial equality.

TRAFFIC – SHARMILA MCNULTY-SHARMA

Jaina's mumma never had much money
Not after papa died
So when Jaina grew to be honest and true,
Her mumma was filled with pride.

Jaina worked hard every day
Making atta for mumma to cook
Her liquorice hair braided down her brown, young back
And by her side a western book.

So when the pretty women came to mumma
They spoke of a desirable land
One that Jaina had read of before
Of money, success and demand.

How beautiful Jaina is
They said, and,
How much money she'll make
She'll come with us to the western world
To refuse would be a mistake.
***

Mumma never saw Jaina again
But Jaina had many visits a night
With no language, her tongue was tied
And nowhere she could run and hide,

Only her body had stories to tell
Of violent dreams and stolen futures.
Foreign corpses in a wishing well.

LEWIS LATIMER – STUART WHOMSLEY

Lewis Latimer
History has placed you in the dark.
Are we taught about your spark of genius,
the carbon light bulb filament?
That Edison invented the bulb is factual,
but you made it affordable and practical.
And how widely is it known,
you were the draftsman of Bell's telephone.
Someone should give the historians a call,
switch on the light, put it right.
They would have made more of you,
Lewis Latimer, if you had been white.

QUESTION FROM A MATE - JAY SANDHU

Two housemates sat in their gaff, somewhere in the Midlands. The lads had known each other almost all of their lives. They weren't just house, they were best mates. After a few games of FIFA, a few ciders and some rums. The chats, as always, moved into the kitchen...

```
             You need to stop,
   be the other definition of differentiate
     Ascertain what makes some different.
     Change during the process of growth
                and development
```

Yo bro where are you from?

                                Like round Mapperley, you know that

Nah, like where are you from?

                                I was born in Derby init, thought you knew that

No bro. Where are you really from???

    (I paused, knowing what he wanted, but not knowing if I should give it)

Like you know, where are you from, from?

    Nah I'm sick of it all the time. You don't care you, think you eat jerk cause you dip reggae reggae

Nah bro it's not that deep, just tell me where you are from

    You don't wanna know about my Kirpan, my sword or my wordplay
        Things like this make some of us downplay

Our heritage disappears quick like exponential decay

*There's just so many of you I don't wanna say something and offend **your** kind*

What does it matter? You won't even notice the difference
Like you're bothered if I pick the pulled pork or the steak
Or how many times a day I pray

For fuck sake, you're all the same, I only asked a question. You're moving like your life is at stake!

Nah it's not even that, it's the assuming; the bias; the judging; towards not even my race
Blaming me for Al-Qaeda and ISIS like I should've caught a case

Bro ain't no one blaming you for that shit

Yeah not you, but I've had plenty of shit thrown at me, sometimes literally

But they're idiots, doesn't even make sense for how could've you been in that cockpit?!

You get me unless I'm wolverine or something. Serious though it's hard to heal with that constant negativity

You always joke about it though, brush it off with bare wit

Of course. I do that deliberately, at that moment what can I do; act timidly? Show my irritability?

Serious?! Yo next time, you know I'll back you! Tell them idiots about it

Trust I know you would, but I've been getting this since
seven, ain't nuttin' change.
Unless people are going to willingly

*Yeah, yeah - there's got to be a bunch willing? I know there's
bare twats but how can we flip it?*

The deeper issue is man don't even realise they are doing it.
That shit is so ingrained in society
We need a major shift and quick

*Alright alright, I get you, but I've not said anything bad...
right?!*

You never directly, but those unconscious micro-aggressions
help accentuate

How can I help? I don't want to be part of society's blight?!

Fighter of justice, dark knight, that you yeah? I'm joking,
step one educate

Then I stop the spread? Then I might understand?

Spread love not judgement or hate, that you need to
habituate

Just having the conversation got me feeling contrite...

You might be finally getting it

```
You need to stop,
be the other definition of differentiate
Ascertain what makes some different.
Change during the process of growth
and development.
```

HEY WHITE BOY – DAVID FRY
(a message to myself)

Hey, white boy.
Don't fear what you don't know.
Fear what you think you know
Cos, they only taught you half the story bro.

Like Churchill, conveniently without his white supremacy
His prejudice and political inhumanity.

The slave trade, ending at abolition
Didn't you know?
Everything's been rosy since emancipation,
Civil rights just a footnote in an uninspiring lesson.

The triangular trade
What? is this a geometry problem?
Maybe we should calculate
How many wretched bodies we can tessellate
Top to tail, face to feet
In the stench and the heat
No air
No hope
Destined only for pain
For suffering
To build the houses and grand estates
To work the fields
Lining the pockets of those whose great,
Great,
Great,
Grandchildren, still own the halls of power
In this, our free and noble nation.

Don't fear what you don't know.

Fear what you think you know.
Fear your arrogant certainty,
Your apathy, naivety,
Cos your conditioned responses
Will most certainly
Corrode your humanity, your credibility.
They will shut down your ears and your empathy
Until you are just another brick in the foundations
On the wrong side of history.

What you think you know
But you don't know,
Will perpetuate the pain
Of those you call sister and brother
Of those whom all too recently
You claimed not to see
Cos you thought that was PC.
You thought that artificial blindness
Was where equality lay,
As if privileged affectations could ever
Conjure up anything more
Than a facsimile of justice.

Examine what you think you know
And be afraid
Of your potential
To do nothing.

"COLOUR BLIND" – HAZEL WARREN

I was raised blind
or partially sighted
didn't have the perspective
of your angles
My vista...
I was raised blind
taught to be good
and thoughtful
and kind it's true
But simply could not see
what was hidden from me
The alternative view
hiding in plain sight, perhaps
noticeable only by its absence
you might say
I was raised blind
and without a home
yet thinking all the world was mine
taking for granted that
I'd find my likeness there
That invisible hands
had designed to meet my needs
Blind to those it excluded
Ignorant to stories not told to me

An innocent, well-meaning kind of ignorance
But ignorance all the same
the only word to describe this deficit
The very act of which makes me complicit
I was raised blind
But now I'm trying to prize open my eyes

We used to think
that you could expand your worldview
with travel - to exotic climes
or that mind-bending psychedelics
would open the doors of perception
But I think really, it's conversations
and stories
and personal connections
that hold the key

I was raised blind
But I'm lifting heavy eyelids
and squinting through keyholes
Using curiosity
to build my empathy
and it's overwhelming
and I know I'm only glimpsing
what you clearly see
But I'm going to try
I was raised blind
But I want to see.

EDUCATION – JAY SANDHU

When I was a kid, I never saw me reflected in a teacher,
Not only was history whitewashed, so was the teacher,
Now I'm a teacher, still ain't seen me reflected in another teacher,
Let alone as a senior leader,
Sometimes when I'm stood in front of a class, I feel like a preacher,
Expand their mind, I thought that was my role, not only a maths teacher,
A kid mentioned race, religion or politics, I'm the guy that stops the algebra and gets a bit deeper,
I've been in all sorts of schools, trust the kids are all the same,
Ok maybe not all, some have already been corrupted by age of eleven,
It's always money and greed,
Sometimes shotting and weed,
Other times it's not wanting to need,
More and more it's hearts on a screen,
Occasionally it's moving mad on lean,
It's becoming a rarity to find a kid that's actually keen,
None of them can imagine spudding their teacher and saying seen.

In all fairness why would they?
They can go viral and make a mint in like a day.
But they only see the glitz and glamour,
Only the highlights not behind the scenes,
I taught a YouTuber, her life looked bless,
30k subscribers and that,
Behind the screens, she's stress,
Sometimes a breakdown, sometimes she's a mess,
She was smashing it;

But realised it was taking a toll,
Told me she remembered something I said,
Didn't even remember it, maybe it's something I read,
Will it bother you in 5 days? Weeks? Months? Bout years?
What's the point in doing something if every week it reduces you to tears,

Shit, my bad I got side-tracked,
My bro gave me the title of education,
I hope you were listening and got educated,
I could spit about policies, education, opportunities and how to make them,
Not only that you have gotta take them,
Privileged mother fuckers get it handed, you gotta fight,
You haven't revised for 4 years, now you gotta do it all night,
But don't worry I've seen it before, graft you'll be alright,
Remember it might not be at 16, maybe later,
Can you imagine, a school system in which, just the elite they don't cater to,
Even without the system stacked in your favour,
I know you'll move to something greater,
Put the imagination to use, maybe you'll be a creator?
Imagine all the teachers not acting snappy like a gator,
Imagine teachers learning collaboratively not like a dictator
Just remember when you made the decision,
Don't flip and give up on that revision,
Complete one goal, celebrate, then set another,
Don't live your life full of coulda, woulda, should haves

THE END – GRAHAM LOCK

Nothing to say
I am white, I stand condemned

Nothing to say,
I am male, I stand condemned

Nothing to say,
I am English, I stand condemned

Trapped between history and despair
This silence is my final guilt

THANKS - JAY SANDHU

The only way to end this incredible collection is to thank the people that made it needed and more importantly, possible.

So...

Thank you, Boris Johnson
Thank you, Donnie Trump
Thank you, Nigel Farage
Thank you, Matt Handcunt
Thank you, Priti Patel
Thank you to those that refuse to be educated
Thank you #AllLivesMatters (except immigrants and those in dinghies)
Thank you to those that wanted the slave owners to stay standing
Thank you EDL-ers
Thank you BNP-ers
Thank you, abusers
Thank you, idiots
Thank you #HorsesLivesMatter (but the 'I'm not vegans')
Thank you, racists
Thank you, misogynists
Thank you, homophobes
Thank you, for being the unneeded opposition
Thank you...No actually fuck you
Fuck all of you, for being the half of the world I want to see burn
You're the ones making the world a worse place for future generations

- - - - - - - -

On a serious,
Thank you to everyone supporting this
Thank you to everyone reading this
Thank you to everyone passing this book to a mate
Thank you to everyone teaching off the curriculum while expanding minds
Thank you to everyone fighting uphill battles every day
Thank you to everyone that wants to educate
Thank you to everyone striving for change
Thank you to everyone who relentlessly fight for the right thing
Thank you to everyone that refuses to stop until things are different

Jay Sandhu - @Sandhuwrites

Nottingham-based Jay Sandhu is a comedian, writer and poet. Punchy, informative and witty, his poetry and comedy focus on race and culture. He has had multiple spoken-word pieces for the BBC, one of which launched a mental health project for young people. Jay is also part of the GOBS Spoken Word Collective and has performed at Bradford, Brighton and Edinburgh Fringe. He has also headlined Late Stage Comedy, and Poetry Scum. You can keep up to date with everything he is doing at linktr.ee/sandhuwrites

Jaya Gordon-Moore - @JayaHadaDream

Born in Cambridge, Jamaican-Irish, JayaHadADream is a female independent rapper, singer and producer. Her music is a merge of thought-provoking, storytelling lyrics with smooth, soulful hip-hop beats. Reaching new heights with her articulate cadence and melodic sound, she has performed across the UK and worked with artists worldwide. Additionally, Jaya uses her academic work in social sciences alongside her passion in music to teach, create and facilitate community arts projects.

Kerion Higgs - @keironhiggspoet

Keiron Lee Higgins, a mixed-race Halifax denizen, started his journey into spoken word territories in 2013, taking inspiration from John Cooper Clarke and Charles Bukowski. Disillusioned in his late 20s with spending nights lugging heavy bags of vinyl and CDs before playing to audiences in local bars as part of a Leeds based Soul and Reggae, a new career was needed in-between juggling his actual job throughout the week. Having several published works including Rebel With a Prose, The Punk With A Northern Soul, Halifax and adoration of records, culminating in headlining a stage at The Halifax Festival Of Words.

Aaalia Zorko - @amzorko

Aalia is a spoken word artist and actor from Nottingham. Having written poetry since the age of 13, but not knowing what to do with it, she joined the GOBs collective at the age of 19 and has been creating and sharing her poetry ever since. Performing at Nottingham Poetry Festival, being a part of BBC Words First, and being chosen to perform at Beatfreeks' 8th Birthday Special of Poetry Jam is among several of her recent achievements.

Andrew Martin

Andrew Martin is a poet with strong political beliefs and an environmental and social conscience. He is a writer of many flavours, often funny, sometimes serious, but always open to new ways of looking at the world. Andrew published his first poetry collection 'Echoes of My Mind' in 2018 and performed with Nottingham DIY Poets at the Edinburgh Fringe in 2019.

Andrea (Annie) Alleyne

Annie Alleyne is a Nottingham based poet originally from Surrey. She is a founding member of the Gobs spoken-word collective. She has performed at Nottingham Poetry Festival and local open mic nights and poetry events; her poetry is featured in the Nottingham C.A.N anthology 'I come from a country where...'. Annie writes deeply personal thought-provoking poetry that stirs emotions.

Hazel Warren - @Hazeleypoos

Hazel Warren is a member of the DIY poets and Paper Cranes collectives. She is an organiser of the International Women's Day event Women Say... Stuff. She has performed her poems in cafes, pubs, bottle shops, book shops and festivals. Hazel has been published in the Best of DIY collections and online by Burning House Press www.burninghousepress.com. Her debut collection To See the Moon is available from Big White Shed www.bigwhiteshed.co.uk. You can contact her (and see pictures of her cat) on Instagram.

Ferzana Shan

Ferzana is a Nottingham poet and radio presenter. She has contributed to several poetry collections and anthologies such as "For the Love of Derbyshire", coal mining anthology "Songs and Rhymes from East Midlands Mines". Ferzana writes her musings as a British Pakistani. She has recently launched 'Ferzana's Poetic Art', an Arts Council funded project.

Kirsty Kelly-Lewin

Kirsty is a Nottingham based spoken word poet. She explores issues of mental health, addiction, suicide, and social care injustices. Her work to date is personal, honest, hard-hitting, and raw. She's a regular ranter at Nottingham's Poetry Scum and Truth Mental Health events. She recently published three of her poems in Nottingham's Community Artists Network 'I Come From A Mind What...' anthology. When she's not voicing the vile and the vulnerable, she loves to attend to her alter ego and spew a good wedding speech full of all things funny, funky and filled with love!

Sharmila McNulty-Sharma - @irisepoetry

Sharmila is a teacher of English, a mother and has also been a young carer. She is from a mixed heritage background, which is reflected in her poetry. Writing poetry was one of Sharmila's hobbies from childhood. The poems Sharmila has written for the RACE collection are based on personal experience: living in a deprived area of Leicester; growing up with an awareness of racial and sexual violence and being a teacher of vulnerable young people. Her favourite poem that she wrote for the RACE collection is Eutopia, as she feels it provides a sense of hope and perhaps an ideal to work towards.

Raisa Saghir - @raisa1s

Raisa is a young and enthusiastic creative, studying Creative Writing for Media Production, involved in Drama, Writing and Modelling. She loves being in front of the camera and has worked with Adam Richards (Power Rangers) and Binde Johal (Harry Potter). Raisa is currently working with another poet from Derby to publish her own anthology, having already had pieces published in the Knitters Museum. She uses writing to help with depression and helps channel her creative energy to create art as a form of expression, showing her personality.